CUT OUT ALONG THE DOTTED LINE & AROUND EACH ENVELOPE LINER

CUT OUT ALONG THE DOTTED LINE & AROUND EACH ENVELOPE LINER

CUT OUT ALONG THE DOTTED LINE & AROUND EACH ENVELOPE LINER

CUT OUT ALONG THE DOTTED LINE & AROUND EACH ENVELOPE LINER

CUT OUT ALONG THE DOTTED LINE & AROUND EACH ENVELOPE LINER

CUT OUT ALONG THE DOTTED LINE & AROUND EACH ENVELOPE LINER

CUT OUT ALONG THE DOTTED LINE & AROUND EACH ENVELOPE LINER